Our Hope

30 Days of God's Promises

Natasha Boehner

outskirts
press

Contents

Day 1: God promises to *fight for us.*

"The Lord will fight for you; you need only to be still." - Exodus 14:14

God promises to *fight for us.*

We don't have to fight our own battles. God promises us that He is always fighting for us and will never stop. Often, we don't get to see what He is doing; instead, He asks us to trust Him and allow Him to do the work. When frustrations arise, accusations occur, or someone hurts us, God tells us to be still and allow him to orchestrate the solution. His ways are always the best ways. Be still, be patient, and be amazed at what He can do in our lives. Let's step back, move aside, and let God fight for us.

Day 2: God promises to *give us wisdom*.

"**If any of you lacks wisdom, you should ask God, who gives generously to all without finding fault, and it will be given to you.**" - James 1:5

God promises to *give us wisdom*.

God promises to give us wisdom in every aspect of our lives. There is nothing too small or unimportant that God doesn't want to talk to us about. When we are feeling stressed or unsure, God promises to help us make wise choices. We are never alone in our decisions. We just need to be still, and pray. Our Father longs to talk with us and guide us. Instead of barreling through the day, take the time to talk with God. His wisdom is too valuable to miss.

Day 3: God promises to *give us strength* when we are weary.

"He gives power to the weak and strength to the powerless."
- Isaiah 40:29

God promises to *give us strength* when we are weary.

God doesn't tell us that he will take away our weakness. Instead, God promises that he will give us strength in our weakness. Strength is the ability to endure. It gives us the ability to stand firm and persevere in the hardest of times. God gives us the strength through prayer and scripture. However, often our strength comes from past hardships God has already walked us through. It is through these hardships that God develops our faith and teaches us how to be strong in Him instead of trying to find the strength within ourselves. God promises that when we feel weary, He will give us the strength to stand firm. One of my favorite verses says it perfectly (Hebrews 12:12): "So take a new grip with your tired hands and strengthen your weak knees." He is our Hope, our Strength, and our Savior.

Day 4: God promises to *never leave us*; He is with us wherever we go.

"Have I not commanded you? Be strong and courageous. Do not be afraid; do not be discouraged, for the Lord your God will be with you wherever you go." - Joshua 1:9

God promises *to never leave us*; He is with us wherever we go.

God walks with us throughout our day. We are never left alone! He wraps his protective wings around us when we feel anxious. He holds our hand to support us when we step out in faith. He stands in front of us and makes it known to the enemy that we are His kid. He sits with us when we feel lonely and sad. He is so faithful and gracious that even when we turn our backs to Him in anger or pride, He won't leave us. He just patiently waits for us to notice Him yet again.

Day 5: God promises to *give us freedom* from the bondage of sin.

"It is for freedom that Christ has set us free. Stand firm, then, and do not let yourselves be burdened again by a yoke of slavery." - Galatians 5:1

God promises to *give us freedom* from the bondage of sin.

We never have to carry around the weight of our mistakes or be a slave to our sins. Jesus promises us He has already taken them from us. There is no sin or temptation that God hasn't given us power over, and there is no sin too great for God's forgiveness. God promises that once we humble ourselves before God, He can see our sin no more.

Day 6: God promises *to protect us*.

"When you pass through the waters, I will be with you, and when you pass through the rivers, they will not sweep over you. When you walk through the fire, you will not be burned; the flames will not set you ablaze." - Isaiah 43:2

God promises *to protect us*.

God promises us that although we may walk through fires that threaten to burn us, be pulled by a swift river that tries to take us downstream, or find ourselves in deep waters struggling to stay afloat, our God promises that we will be under his protective care the entire time. Because no matter what, He promises VICTORY.

Day 7: God promises *to make good out of the bad* situations of our lives.

"And we know that God causes everything to work together for the good of those who love God and are called according to his purpose for them." - Romans 8:28

God promises *to make good out of the bad* situations of our lives.

God promises us that although we will walk through deep waters and face many struggles on this earth, if we submit to Him, He can and will make good out of all of our pain and suffering. We may not see it today, and sometimes we have to leave it to faith, but God doesn't waste our pain. He loves to take our trials and give purpose to them.

Day 8: God promises *to always be available* to us.

"Ask and it will be given to you; seek and you will find; knock and the door will be opened for you." - Matthew 7:7

God promises to always be available to us.

God is available to us every minute of the day. If we pray, He will bend down to listen. If we read, He will teach. If we ask, He will guide. He is available 24/7 to hear and answer every prayer we utter. In all circumstances big and small, God is listening. God loves when we can quiet ourselves and be still so we can hear Him whisper back.

Day 9: God promises *to love us unconditionally*.

"**For the mountains may move and the hills disappear, but even then, my faithful love for you will remain. My covenant of blessing will never be broken, says the Lord, who has mercy on you.**" - Isaiah 54:10

God promises *to love us unconditionally*.

God promises us that no matter how many times we mess up, His love for us is unchanging. We can't earn His love through good works. He, in the truest sense, loves us unconditionally. God meets us with open arms in our anger, disobedience, selfishness, pride, and even when we lack faith. It's Agape love! What a gift!

Day 10: God promises *to give us Joy*.

"These things I have spoken to you, that my joy may be in you, and that your joy may be made full." - John 15:11

God *promises to give us Joy*.

God doesn't give us all the things we think will make us happy. He doesn't promise health, marriage, kids, money, and comfort. Instead, He promises us JOY in all circumstances if we abide in Him. You see, the Lord's plans are deeper and far more satisfying than the plans we see for ourselves. God promises us that if we keep looking up and hanging out with Him, we will experience the kind of JOY that is deep, rich, and sustaining, even when OUR hopes and desires seem to be wavering.

Day 11: God promises us that He has *made us courageous*.

"For God has not given us a spirit of fear and timidity, but of power, love and self-discipline." - 2 Timothy 1:7

God promises us that He has *made us courageous*.

God promises us that he has made us to be brave and courageous. We don't have to be fearful and timid. God tells us that we have an inner Spirit, the Holy Spirit, that makes us strong and fearless. God often asks us to step out in faith and do things we don't think we can do. But with the help of the Holy Spirit, we can do them. We never have to doubt that we have the ability to perform the tasks God asks of us. All we need to do is trust in God's promise that He has already equipped us, and when the time is right, the Holy Spirit will give us the confidence, strength, and exact skills needed to perform anything God is calling us up to do. The best part is that each time we see God do this in our lives, we also see our Faith grow bigger each and every time.

Day 12: God promises *to give us rest.*

"Come to me, all you who are weary and burdened, and I will give you rest. Take my yoke upon you and learn from me, for I am gentle and humble in heart, and you will find rest for your souls." - Matthew 11: 28-29

God promises *to give us rest.*

God promises that when we are feeling weary and stressed, He will give us rest. Sometimes life has us feeling emotionally exhausted. It's at these times God tells us that we don't have to handle it all alone; He will come alongside of us. He will join us in our struggle. He opens his arms and tells us to give Him our burdens, our doubts, our stress, and in return he will give us rest. God doesn't want us to carry the burdens of this world. God wants to renew, refresh, and encourage our spirits. So, he says, "Come to me, with all of your burdens, and I will give you rest."

Day 13: God promises *us* *Eternal life*.

"And this is what he promised us—eternal life." - 1 John 2:25

God promises *us* *Eternal life*.

God tells us that our time here on earth is short. The love and beauty of this world is only a tiny glimpse of the love and beauty yet to come. We don't need to gobble up all that this life offers because God has promised us so much more—an eternal life so amazing we can't even comprehend it. Real joy comes when our focus is on serving our Father. We are living on a battlefield and WE are God's army. What good is an army if it's not participating in the battle? God wants us to be his hands and feet and tend to his flock. God promises us that in only a short time we will be reunited with those who have served already and have gone home to wait for us. He promises us that in our eternal life, there will be no more pain and no more suffering. So, rest in his promise of eternal life and be a good soldier because we know we already have victory.

Day 14: God promises to *provide us with the self-discipline we need to fight temptations.*

"The temptations in your life are no different from what others experience. And God is faithful. He will not allow the temptation to be more than you can stand. When you are tempted, he will show you a way out so that you can endure." - 1 Corinthians 10:13

God promises to *provide us with the self-discipline we need to fight temptations.*

We all have things in our lives we have difficulty saying "no" to. These are generally things that have become idols in our lives and give us false comfort. If we are honest, often they are things God has been asking us to set aside, but we instead choose to hold on to them. We simply have made the choice to ignore God's guidance and choose our own path. Often, we will try to use willpower to fight against our temptations. However, willpower is really just a quick fix. God tells us that He has given us the "Holy Spirit" that will provide all we need to fight against temptation if we choose to activate it. If we can bring God alongside of us and give Him our full attention, we will find we no longer feel the need to run back to those tempting idols. We cannot be tempted by things we no longer desire. When our desire for God gets deeper and deeper, our longing for the things of this world will become less and less important. God doesn't ask us to rely on sheer willpower. God promises us that when we are tempted, He will show us a way out so that we can endure and find His path to freedom.

Day 15: God promises that He *will carry our burdens for us*.

"Give your burdens to the Lord, and he will sustain you, he will never let the righteous be shaken." - Psalm 55:22

God promises that He will *carry our burdens for us*.

God doesn't want us to shoulder our burdens. Instead, He tells us to cast all of our troubles to Him. HE will carry them for us. What a good Father he is! He promises to always take care of us, because we are His kids! He knows exactly what we need and the best way to provide for us. In fact, He knows far better than we do what is best. We don't need to be anxious or fearful. We don't need to worry about tomorrow because no matter what our day looks like, God is walking with us, eager and ready to carry all of our heavy baggage.

Day 16: God promises to *give us peace*.

"Don't worry about anything; instead, pray about everything. Tell God what you need, and thank Him for all He has done. Then you will experience God's peace, which extends beyond anything we can understand." - Philippians 4:6-7

God promises to *give us peace*.

Jesus is the Prince of Peace. He promises that if we pray, exercise faith, live by his guidance, and love one another, we will have peace. Peace comes from the Holy Spirit. When we are living in God's presence, we keep things in perspective, looking at things through God's eyes. Taking God's perspective also guides our reactions to those around us, bringing great peace to our relationships and day-to-day experiences. Peace is not the absence of problems; rather it's the presence of God in our lives. If we abide in Him, He promises to give us peace.

Day 17: God promises to *comfort us*.

"All praise to God, the Father of our Lord Jesus Christ. God is our merciful Father and the source of all comfort. He comforts us in all our troubles so that we can comfort others. When they are troubled, we will be able to give them the same comfort God has given us." - 2 Corinthians 1 3-4

God promises to *comfort us*.

God promises us that He will always be with us to comfort us. He strengthens, encourages, and stands by us when we are struggling. He listens to our cries and sits with us when we are hurting. He may bring encouragement through a friend, or give us that perfect song that says exactly what we need to hear. Often, He gives us a verse that rekindles our hope. Because He is our Father, He knows exactly how to comfort us. What is so amazing, though, is that God's comfort circulates among us and often the comforting comes full circle. You see, God comforts us and then asks us to comfort others. What a blessing!

Day 18: God promises to *bless us*.

"You parents—if your children ask for a loaf of bread, do you give them a stone instead? Or if they ask for fish, do you give them a snake? Of course not! So, if you sinful people know how to give good gifts to your children, how much more will your heavenly Father give good gifts to those who ask him."
- Matthew 7:9-11

God promises to *bless us*.

God promises to bless us in our obedience and will even bless us when we are not. He is our loving Father and wants to give us the desires of our heart. But like a good father, there are times He knows best, and what is best may not be what our hearts cry out for. However, even in difficult times God will graciously pour out His blessing in ways we may not even see. There are also natural blessings that come when we are obedient, forgiving, gracious, giving, and loving. Blessings also come when we spend time in worship and His word. Most importantly, though, God blesses us so that we can bless others, and the more we bless others, the more God will bless us. You see, our blessings are not for us to hold on to; the real blessings come when we can pass them on.

Day 19: God *promises us grace.*

"For sin shall no longer be your master, because you are not under the law, but under grace." - Romans 6:14

God *promises us grace.*

God promises us that He never keeps score. There is nothing we can do that will make Him love us any less. His grace is perfect and pure. Once we humble ourselves and confess our sins, God can see the sin no more. Sin no longer needs to be our master. We don't have to slay it, escape it, or make up for it. WE are free! It is His promise to us. When we see all that God has forgiven us for, it empowers us to extend that same grace to others. God asks us to free others we are holding in chains of our own anger and hurt. In God's perfect plan, He knows that by extending grace to others, our hearts will be clean. God knows a clean heart is one filled with joy, peace, and love.

Day 20: God promises to *take care of our needs*.

"Therefore, do not be anxious, saying, 'What shall we eat?' or 'What shall we drink?' or 'What shall we wear?' For the Gentiles seek after all these things, and your heavenly Father knows that you need them all." - Matthew 6:31-32

God promises to *take care of our needs*.

God knows exactly what we need, and he wants us to look to Him to be our provider. God doesn't want us to carry physical, spiritual, or emotional burdens. Instead, he tells us to bring all of our cares to Him. Luke 12:13 says to "Seek the kingdom of God above all else, and He will give you everything you need." God wants us to let Him take care of tomorrow so we can serve Him today.

Day 21: God promises to *restore and redeem us*.

"And the God of all grace, who called you to His eternal glory in Christ, after you have suffered a little while, will himself restore you and make you strong, firm and steadfast." - 1 Peter 5:10

God promises to *restore and redeem us*.

When God sees us, He sees our heart. He sees who we can become and who He created us to be. He never sees who we once were. He delights in taking all of the broken pieces of our heart: the shame, the anger, the hurt, the insecurity and the pain, and restoring them to something beautiful. His light shines even brighter when it is illuminated with the reflection of our brokenness. He repairs, redeems, renovates, and then reinstates us to serve Him with a stronger faith, a reshaped character, and the grace and empathy to truly understand and serve others. No matter what we have done or what has been done to us, God promises us that He can and will restore and redeem us to an even higher standing if we just take His hand.

Day 22: God promises that He created us for a *purpose and has given us special gifts.*

"For we are God's handiwork, created in Christ Jesus to do good works, which God prepared in advance for us to do." - Ephesians 2:10:

"Each of you should use whatever gift you have received to serve others, as faithful stewards of God's grace in its various forms." - 1 Peter 4:10:

God promises that He created us for *a purpose and has given us special gifts.*

God knows the most intimate parts of our hearts because He formed us and handpicked everything from our noses to our toes. He created our personalities, even our quirks. We are fearfully and wonderfully made in God's image. No mistakes. God created us each individually different because He has a specific purpose for each one of us. God gives us unique talents and spiritual gifts to use to bless others and serve Him. We have great value to God, but sometimes it's hard for us to see the beautifully unique person He created us to be.

Day 23: God promises that *if we seek Him we will find Him*.

"But from there you will search again for the Lord your God. And if you search for Him with all your heart and soul, you will find Him." - Deuteronomy 4:29:

"Draw near to God and he will draw near to you." - James 4:8:

God promises that if we seek Him we will find Him.

We were created to long for our Father. Our souls ache when we distance ourselves from God. "As the deer pants for streams of water, so my soul pants for you" (Psalm 42:1). God will love us through our anger, disappointment, and sorrow. He graciously and patiently waits for us to turn our eyes to Him. When we are ready, He draws us into His heavenly arms. God loves us so much that even when we try to stand alone, He promises us that if and when we seek Him, we will find Him. He will never desert us.

Day 24:God promises us that *He will baptize us with the Holy Spirit.*

"Deep calls to deep in the roar of your waterfalls; all your waves and breakers have swept over me." - Psalm 42:1

"When the Advocate comes, whom I will send to you from the Father—the Spirit of truth who goes out from the Father—He will testify about me." - John 15:26

God promises us that He will baptize us with the Holy Spirit.

The Holy Spirit is an amazing gift. It comforts us, renews us, gives us joy and peace. It guides us against temptations, assists us in prayer, and teaches us. The Holy Spirit is in sweet fellowship and communion with our Father. In its purest form, the deep areas of our spirit connect to the deep things of God. It is a special time of intimacy between a Father and a Child. When God calls us out to deep waters, He asks us to seek Him; when deep calls to deep, an intimate encounter with our Father refreshes our souls and breathes new life into us.

Day 25: God promises that *He will never Forsake us*.

"No one will be able to stand against you all the days of your life. As I was with Moses, so I will be with you; I will never leave you nor forsake you." - Joshua 1:5

God promises that He will never Forsake us.

God promises that no matter what mistakes we make, situations we face, or sin we commit, He will never abandon us, turn away from us, or leave us behind. In this life, at some point, we will be forsaken by people we care about. Even Jesus knew what it felt like to be abandoned. Jesus walked an agonizing journey to the cross all alone, forsaken and betrayed by those He loved. God wants us to know that we never have to fear that from Him. He wants us to stand strong in our faith knowing that He is **always** for us and never against us. No matter what, we have His assurance that He will NEVER abandon us.

Day 26: God promises that *HE is all we need.*

"And my God will meet all your needs according to the riches of this glory in Christ Jesus." - Philippians 4:19

God promises that HE is all we need.

God promises that we don't need to find our comfort, wisdom, security, love, peace, or even joy in the things of this world. Our Father is a Great Provider. There is nothing we need physically, emotionally, or spiritually that He can't provide for us. God asks us to faithfully place all of our idols at His feet. He wants us to trust Him with our "everything" because He is the Alpha and Omega, the Great I Am! We need Him as much as we need our every breath.

Day 27: God promises that *He has equipped us and will protect us from the evil one.*

"Put on the full armor of God, so that you can take your stand against the devil's schemes." - Ephesians 6:11:

"But the Lord is faithful, and He will strengthen you and protect you from the evil one." - 2 Thessalonians 3:3:

God promises that He has equipped us and will protect us from the evil one.

God is Sovereign over Satan; however, until Jesus comes back for us, Satan has been allowed to deceive us, accuse us, and lead us to sin. The good news, though, is that if we are a child of God, we do not have to live in fear of the enemy. God knows we will be refined in our faith through our battles with the enemy. But as a protective Father, he doesn't send us into battle without providing all we need to stand strong and resist the enemy. God gives us the belt of Truth to shut down Satan's lies. He gives us the breastplate of righteousness to help us obey God. The Sandals of Peace help us to carry the light of God. The Helmet of Salvation gives us hope. The Shield of Faith lets us trust. The Sword of the Spirit gives us the power.

God is sculpting us to be skilled soldiers on this spiritual battlefield. But He promises we have His protection and all of the weapons we need to be victorious. In fact, He has already told us, WE win. But God still has much for us to do, so He reminds us to put on The Armor of God and get back at it.

Day 28: God promises *to be* our refuge.

"He will cover you with his feathers, and under His wings you will find refuge; his faithfulness will be your shield and rampart." - Psalm 91:4

God promises to be our refuge.

There is no situation that is out of God's control. Wrapped in His loving arms is the safest place to always be. Even though God is in control, He tells us that there will be difficult times for us as we walk through this life on earth. During these difficult days, sometimes God will swoop in and rescue us. But most often, God puts His protective wing around us, asks us to have faith, and walks through it with us. God is our refuge in all situations if we are in the center of His will. He is faithful, He is our safe place, He is our strength when we feel weak.

Day 29: God promises *His word will always produce fruit.*

"The rain and snow come down from the heavens and stay on the ground to water the earth. They cause the grain to grow, producing seed for the farmer and bread for the hungry. It is the same with my word. I send it out, and it always produces fruit. It will accomplish all I want it to, and it will prosper everywhere I send it." - Isaiah 55:10-11

God promises His word will always produce fruit.

A faithfully watered seed produces food that feeds our physical bodies. The word of God, when faithfully studied, is what feeds our soul. The Bible is a powerful tool that God uses to teach us, convict us, comfort us, and arm us with His Truth. It is God's living word, our manual; it will guide us down the narrow road that leads to abundant life. God promises that if we pick up His tool every day, we will be blessed and produce much fruit.

Day 30: God promises that *He is faithful always*.

"If we are unfaithful, He remains faithful, for He cannot deny who He is." - 2 Timothy 2:13

God promises that He is faithful always.

God has a firm allegiance to us that cannot be broken. God never lies, is always loyal, and stands firm. His words are always true; God is the same today as He was yesterday. "Heaven and earth will disappear, but My words will remain forever" (Luke 21:33). Every time we step out in faith, we learn of God's faithfulness. When God gives us a promise, He is faithful always. Even when WE are unfaithful, God's commitment to us never wavers. With faith, we can stand firm and steadfast on all of God's promises knowing He is faithful and His love for us is unchanging.

CPSIA information can be obtained
at www.ICGtesting.com
Printed in the USA
BVHW032345010219
539300BV00001B/48/P